DATE DUE

Demco, Inc. 38-293

NOV 1 2 2009

THE PACIFIC NORTHWEST POETRY SERIES

Linda Bierds, General Editor

THE PACIFIC NORTHWEST POETRY SERIES

SECOND NATURE

POEMS BY JOHN WITTE

University of Washington Press   *Seattle and London*

Second Nature: Poems by John Witte, the eighth volume in the Pacific Northwest Poetry Series, is published with the generous support of Cynthia Lovelace Sears.

© 2008 by the University of Washington Press
Printed in the United States of America
Designed by Ashley Saleeba
12 11 10 09 08   5 4 3 2 1
First edition 2008

University of Washington Press
P.O. Box 50096, Seattle, WA 98145 U.S.A.
www.washington.edu/uwpress

Library of Congress Cataloging-in-Publication Data
Witte, John, 1948-
Second nature : poems / by John Witte. — 1st ed.
p. cm. — (Pacific Northwest poetry series ; 8)
ISBN 978-0-295-98859-7 (alk. paper)
I. Title.
PS3573.I917S43 2008
811'.54—dc22   2008028668

The paper used in this publication is acid-free and 90 percent recycled from at least 50 percent post-consumer waste. It meets the minimum requirements of American National Standard for Information Sciences—Permanence of Paper for Printed Library Materials, ANSI Z39.48-1984. ∞

Epigraph, p. vii: The poem by George Oppen is from his *Selected Poems*, ed. Robert Creeley (New York: New Directions, 2003).

FOR MY DAUGHTERS, JOSIE AND ANNA

... is it not
In fear the roots grip

Downward
And beget

The baffling hierarchies
Of father and child

—GEORGE OPPEN, "OF BEING NUMEROUS"

CONTENTS

ONE | **ROOTS**

FALLING BLOSSOMS

When the wind
swells through the plum trees
go dreamy loosening their white petals you have to begin

singing not
too loud the bees having
kindled the ovary the flower done now dappling the air

like moths
fluttering you have to imagine
the petals swirling down a sudden flurry of confetti

settling on
a child at a party the petals
sparkly like fish scales leaping behind the knife a boy

cleaning his catch
scales speckling his plaid shirt
or the splatterings under the ladder of a man painting

his house white
in the failing light the flakes
of ash the perishable stars stinging our face and hands

like memory
itself a heaven-scented residue
gathering at our feet the pale sediment of our lives.

HIS CAP

Why because
he was happy he threw his cap
into the sky over the field behind his house

he picked it up
and tossed it again his unspoken
hooray wobbling through the air people did this at games

when the war
ended they were so glad they
threw their hats it was part of the language of our lives

he was trying to
understand giving another heave
of his cap with its little bill into the blue sky the unseen

celestial matter
making a funny quacking sound
practicing his blatty duck voice his mother calling come in

this minute
leaving his cap in the grass why
because he was warm then with no need of a cap until now.

THAT

That's what
I'm saying how it felt to rise
on the ferris wheel the world war over the seat rocking

making a shrill
chirping I was alone or else
my brother was there already in pain that's what I mean

about memory
climbing up through the salty air
off the Atlantic then sinking into the smell of popcorn

a spattering of vomit
on the platform the mechanism
gasping the worm-gear engaged turning the wheel lifting

our little pew
into the sky or so we thought
dizzy in the breeze smelling of wisteria and stars

that's what I mean
about language that's how the world
was revealed to me in Elizabeth New Jersey at the age

of eight descending
through the smoke of the barbecue pit
the charred meat weeping then rising again into heaven.

FROM

Tulips and windmills
wooden shoes clopping the cobblestones
a boy with his finger in the dike holding back the ocean

that was me
drawing a map of Holland
its wiggly inlets and eleven provinces who can say where

he comes from
a schoolboy studying his family's
country of origin I see now we were ashamed and so I was

a little Dutch
boy like Hans Brinker skating
to school not Poland that war-torn doubtful place it was

the buoyant 50s
after all not children on their knees
rinsing mud from potatoes I leaned close to the paper

erasing and
penciling in the levees and seawalls
the agricultural and dairy and flower-growing regions

it's taking forever
Poland would have been easier
its map a block its artists cruising the shabby avenues

like sharks
but life here in Holland is good
we are a happy people though the sea presses in on us.

THE SOUND BARRIER

The sky boomed
what was it not thunder not
blasting at the quarry the little birds flew up the dog

woofed once
then listened the boy crossing
the field cringed lifting his shoulders the sky spoke

not again not
his father's rage slamming the door
rattling the cupboard the wall cracked the swept-wing

fighters banked
over the airfield plaster falling
from the ceiling not a quake not the end of their lives

not the crump
and concussion of a bomb
a sonic boom passed over the field the cow staggered

into the creek
the eggs cracked in their nest
the boy saluted the mare threw herself on the fence.

SARTRE'S EYE

My first job
a solemn kid at the wheel
the delivery truck full of crashing barricades I was free

frazzled
by the gridlock stopped
at a traffic light in Manhattan but this is not my story

or even the story
of Sartre passing on the crosswalk
close enough to touch the dented grill hardly lifting his

feet moving
through the silt of solitude
parting the cool stream of oncoming pedestrians but about

Sartre's wandering
eye round and watery anxious
glancing sidelong up at me through the cracked windshield

his moon-eye
fixed on me for some time
afterward even now after it is closed seeming to watch me

from the other side
where the awful pressure of
the sea has compressed his body his flounder eye gazing up.

HIS DREAMS

You weren't yourself
from then on ever again he flew
over your car so now you had to have the old man's dreams

a woman waving
her hand bright with duck's blood
the water rising the furniture floating in the rooms he left

without his glasses
crossing the road in the dark you
in your small car coming toward him under the trees must have

seemed to be
farther away than you were skidding
you had the strangest dreams where would they have come from

if not him
a dog chewing a severed hand
a boy driving past the barn the lighted house a burly man

breaking into
a run across the road crumpling
the fender lying curled on his side under an orange blanket

as if asleep
on the shoulder as if to say
it's all right you can go on but you have to have my dreams

otherwise
where will they go the cider horse
the siren approaching the barn collapsing like a human lung.

SWATH

Mint and feathers glint of a can stubble and rubbish I walk
in the clutter of the roadside mower its half-
human growl beyond

a bend the breaking
waves of grass the seat thunking
I know the oily clatter of the cutterbar's reciprocating teeth

I see where he has steered around a log or lifted the bar over
a stump or stone the weeds and seedlings
crowding us pressing in

on the road he may be
alone today or else his son is with him
already in work shirt and overalls enclosed in the coarse shell

of noise a paw
a squirrel in the mower the boy
might want to examine this hash of plastic paper and fur

the turtle's
cracked house the writhing
snake tying its final slipknot he might have something to say.

TICK

Or was it
yesterday climbing the layers of light
and gazing down on the Valley of the West like gods out of time

a tick crab-
walking the miles of my body burrowed
into my hip listening to the heart whine dreaming and drinking

scarab carrier
of messages aches and contagion
little traveler anchored at the mouth by the word blood

bleb or black bird
on a field of snow or this family
story told to remember the forgotten child my mother's mother's

mother's radiant
youngest son voweling in the fire
of scarlet fever his name *Krzysztof* stuck on my tongue the Polish

Communion the church
hushed the soul leaping dear Lord for joy
a boy shuffling the endless aisle to the altar and opening

his mouth how
could they know the fever was passed
on his borrowed clothes the beautiful suit clasping his chest

the wafer
like dust on his tongue
take and eat this ghostly food in remembrance of me.

THE PLEDGE

The children rise
and touch their foreheads their faces
hazy as if through a window grimed with industrial soot we see

what the photographer saw a tenement school the children
shielding their eyes from the flash
I see my father

his tongue pushing
forward the stone of language his head
shaved vague a smudge or slur of light someone slipping

away the words
in chalk the window open to an alley
maybe he was trying to see behind the camera someone

hidden inside
his grown son gazing back at him
saying *Don't worry I'm waiting for you here* under the black

cowl the photographer shuts one eye the faces of those nearest
burned away in the flash I see now
the girl holds a flag

small as a handkerchief on a stick the class is repeating
the pledge he hasn't learned yet
how to salute.

HELICOPTER RIDE

We shrink wakes
of air breaking over us you cannot
hear my voice in the hatta-hatta-hatta of the rotors

huffing the dust
on the fairgrounds the machine
rising under its halo our bodies freeze buffeted

by prop wash
and chuffing like the helicopter we saw
hovering over the river its floodlights searching

the water pleated
petaled like a white chrysanthemum.
My daughter rides the elephant one foot dragging

a shackle and chain
in a circle slow as time in the jungle.
His ears flap. He doesn't mind the racket the dilapidated

chopper crouched
in the hayfield the pilot a vet
gone to seed his shades and blue tattoos his frayed khakis

patched with insignia
we pay and climb in a spinning
at the brainstem lifting us yawing over the barbecue

red and yellow
trees flashing the dirt path
lined with huts the children looking up and running.

INTERROGATION

Tell us
everything you know why and
where were the others and at what point did you realize

who knew
what they had in mind and
when did you notice that he was not who he said he was

and why then
didn't you recognize her voice
you were in deeper than you thought you were afraid yet

earlier you said
he never mentioned it so
what did you think was their reason for placing the call

what happened
when you arrived could you see who
opened the door and how did you know they would know

it was you
and what did you think that
your life so peaceful would continue on as before?

OBIT

Who every so
often who waded into the water
who moved from place to place who imagined his life to be

who took-out
who returned his calls who tried
nevertheless who wanted in all the world nothing more than

who became
uneasy whose mind would not who
felt himself going down that road who thought perhaps now

who gazing
up into the flashing firmament
who spun who winked off and on who tried to remember a time

who spoke but
only to find that whenever he
who seems to have misunderstood who clung to the hope that

who labored and didn't
complain who looked everywhere who
skewed and scribbled who asked but it was not to be given

who got some
airtime who dwindled who
thinned out who came to a door hesitated and opened it.

TWO | **BEGATS**

NEWBORN

You make a sound like a door opening.
You make a sound like talking
in your sleep little one
eye open on the breast
you root and mew and swoon.

Little cry out in the darkness

I remember your first hour on earth.
I remember the anonymous 14th-century
painting of a child in meditation
floating on a lotus blossom.
I remember your mother and I
kept perfectly still your eyes pouring
their deep water into the room.

The blood test was coming
a steel dart stabbing your heel. The cramp
of hunger and the menstrual cramp
the days and nights were coming.

Give us a moment
together in this calm
before the onset of need.

THE SEED

The jade dwarf
smiled or sneered a fetal god
we were young and far from home the terra-cotta wrestlers

grappling the woman
nursing a dog in the shadows a thief
crouched dense fleshy a stubbly spongy muzzle snarling

or was it
a baby mewling curling back
its lip we counted out the heavy coins we could not say

the mellifluous names
of the flowers we were about to lose
and gain everything we did not see the coati darting out

bloodying your ankle
with its teeth we did not know
you were pregnant already in the warm rain

each of the animals
beginning with the smallest
passing through the chamber of your womb.

IRIS INNOMINATA

My boot
slips the trail slick dwindling
in a creamy drift of flowers not lost but momentarily

stumped
among Iris innominata *having no name*
the blossoms maroon-veined the fleshy funnel the swollen

bulb of the ovary
remembering you inside trying
to be born your body caught in the pubic hoop

the umbilical noosed
around your neck your skull
squeezed through that hourglass we held you scuffed

concussed your blue
limbs slathered with mother oil
your eyes black *having an unknown or unrevealed name*

I must remember
the way back past the slumped
shack the rockslide the path meandering into this meadow

half asleep the sky
beginning to darken a doll appearing
in your eye your tiny father grave in the obsidian mirror.

NAMING

A needle piercing
your world the natal fluid sparkled
like champagne in the syringe. A single cell of you
came into focus: the chromosomes the forty-six
angels. We had begun

to call you Anna
the name of a woman with her father's large hands able
to love deeply and openly Anna from Tolstoy
Anna mother of the mother of god.

But today bicycling to work
I passed a yard where someone's belongings were piled
in plastic bags by the curb a woman was turning
away from a man her face

folding inward gathering
like water through a narrow place at the moment before
tears her body sobbed under the loose shift
she was shaking her head *not again*
and turning her back and burying
her face in a dish towel.

Maybe he was wrong
the man holding his hands in midair.
The sun pressed down on him helpless as anyone seeing
the wreck of his life and he said
Anna as I rolled past.

LIKENESS

Hungry, your mother gone
for the afternoon, you touch my chest
the breast recognizable under the hair the nipple
asleep. This is how you strain toward her
and she lifts her blouse and you
woozily open your lips.

We read a book. You understand
from my voice that there is sadness. Someone
is lost in the story
but it will be OK.

During the labor I felt you letting go at last
slipping through the bone gates
into time.

You cry and I open my shirt.
I hold you nuzzling asleep your lips
moving in willing self-deception beside this
rough chest, this inkling
of a breast.

GRACE

Just reading
the Sunday paper strewn on the floor
since you asked we're doing next to nothing the baby and I

skimming famine
floods and war she clucks and chuckles
the space station like a seed pod peeling apart spilling

scanners and spectrographs
clipboards flashlights and playing cards
jumpsuits booties and nippled sacks of pureed food

my daughter
kisses the newlyweds she kneels
on the paper and kisses the man trying to cover his face

with his cuffed
hands her lips smudged she kisses
the baby bundled in rags the father grieving a simple

affection
she kisses the woman
running toward us her house going up in flames.

PALENQUE

Snatching our bag he runs into the jungle catching
his breath he digs through
our belongings

camera apples guidebooks finding our money
and documents he learns our names
he takes the pen

and notebook
the notes for a poem this poem.
We emerge from the Temple of Inscriptions each day

carried forth
by a god or demon the jungle
a tangled dream we wake from and forget the thief

is safe here
he holds the picture of Deb
me and Josie flushed from birth we are his now

hostages
to his poverty his prospects
finally looking up he has the keys to our house

our car
he has my passport my face anxious
in the photo preparing for a journey this journey.

DAYCARE

He was taken
by the rough nude in her garden its green
thigh scribbled with salts the cheeks scabbed and bitten amazed

it was her sculpture
this woman who cared for his daughter
while he was at work staring into the blue screen her gangly

arm almost lost
in the tangled dragnet her chest
crushed a metal wing seeming to jut crumpled from her shoulder.

She would not sell it
to him or anyone. It was not the woman
she wanted. She would recast it if only she could find the time

what with the rain
the ragged grass and the children
vaulting the sofa yelling filling every corner with their music.

She would start again
cooking and pouring the slurry
into the foot and knee seething in the hollow thigh the bronze

flooding up
into her mouth. She would break the mold
and free her if she could. She would make the woman whole.

FUGUE FOR JOSIE

Your first note
a long bow on the E-string a melodic sigh
the afternoon light streams over the audience in gowns and bibs

your school ensemble come to perform at the nursing home.
Famished they devour you the music easy
to grasp their wheelchairs

crowding the chapel like a parking lot. The pure harmonic echo
luminous and colloquial the theme recurring
in memory you lose

and find your place the music a fluid continuum of industry
quick through the passages of grace.
But the odds

are against them
their white smocks and pre-school murmur
the weight of a head dragging its body forward a chair rolls

out of the front row breaking ranks the woman's face rapt
her hand rowing over the wheel
you watch her

mouth open your fingers searching for the strings the chorus
and broken chords her chair gliding
toward you yearning

to be closer
the nurse pushing through to stop her
the joyful crescendo the *cantus firmus* filling the chapel.

ANNA'S HORSES

This might be
the tabernacle. These might be
the instruments of worship my daughter's horses on the bureau

their ears up
she comes murmuring their names
drawing her brush down their muscled flanks. They have a barn

of pastel snap-
together panels but it has never been
assembled. Instead she hammered and glued scraps of splintery

shingles a rickety
shed leaning in the wind.
She loves them and though she thinks she cannot pray prays

for a horse. You see
where this is heading. She stands them
on a snow white sheet of paper and guides her wambly crayon

providing for each
a stall and sketchy bedding a fence
with a gate. They come and go. You can picture it now. Finally

it will be nowhere
but here in the mouth and ear nothing
but words a horse breathing in the first light in the cool

must she nickers
my daughter comes lugging
the saddle and speaks to her plunging tossing her mane.

THE HEAVENLY LADDER

A beauty beyond us
you stroked her sleek withers
raked and shoveled her stall before your lesson I went on

to the library. A cautious
love you seated the bit. I pored over
the brilliantly illuminated miniatures of the eleventh century.

The horse peevish
frisky I learned what happened
later how our lives diverged the jewel-blue water surging

from the left
across the bottom of the picture
the horse buckjumping pitching you up and down your teacher

covering her mouth
with her hands there was nothing
I could do I was not there I was absorbed by the small figure

of a monk gathering
his violet-blue tunic closer
the shimmering golden ladder extending diagonally into the sky

I had to
imagine you lurching side to side
a black curtain falling between you and the spinning world.

You awoke
on your back under the blue arc
of heaven the enormous head of the horse gazing down.

ARK

Spoor stink
thrush song the knobby quick
fingers of a paw digging I open the meat-colored notebook

the sky gathering
over the animals the new owners
stepping over the bones and branches the eggshell skull of a fawn

unscrolling blue-
prints big plans the heavenly
household laughter and crying in the forest a circular stairway

of burned air
climbing over the mired bull-
dozed stumped and gutted clearing a gyring uprush of redtails

placing the entry
here the deck here the house
seeming to tip and pitch in the mind like a boat with many rooms

a deer gazing in
a wing striking the invisible
window the eager gug-gug of a squirrel tearing the shingles

placing the sofa
here the coffee table here
the porch light crusted with an iridescent tissue of mayflies

a child at the threshold
listening to the rain the animals
scuffling in the crawlspace half in our world half in theirs.

AUTO ZOO

Just then
a giraffe stepped into the road
gazing at us through the dusty windshield an ostrich

an elephant swam
in the wavery heat the ark of memory
breached and foundering the animals adrift in our lives

the car crept
like a tortoise through the Heart
of Africa the cheetahs retreating to their tin lean-to

that's when
the engine chunked coughed and
quit there was no one else on the road the rhino watched

the jackal crouched
the lions rose and stretched
the parrot a slash of red the tiger crept toward us.

CLEARCUT

Why this din
these boughs nervous with birds more
descending out of the sky crowding into the last tree

for miles trilling
like a green lathe the crush
and cluster of wings bursting forth circling and plunging

back into the limbs
their only perch they have come
to ease their shoulders before flying on manic clamorous

the craunching
and revving sounds they've learned
traveling among us a feathery host spattering the leaves

a jittery
choir atonal off the hinges
their fierce singing their recognizable desperate psalm.

CAPTIVITY

She holds her breath
she's sick of the goats my daughter says
if they mean so much to you then you feed them she cannot

stand the darkness
in the small barn her father built
the spider webs heavy with dust hanging like torn velour

the slick path
and sloshing water bucket bad enough
the goat thrusting his nose between her legs and now this

wasps' hive
droning in the rafters the gibbering
swallows swerving into their mud gourd nest a rustling

fleshy commotion
inside the stinking billy wagging
his member the brown berries of shit on the straw

once she forgot
to close the gate fearful
they'd run away but there they were contentedly browsing

once she
found a rat fallen into
the plastic grain bin frantically digging in the foot

of food trapped
in its heaven she heard it
squeal scuttling up the sheer walls and falling back.

THE OCEAN

Swabs of
orange and grayish-purple
my daughter's first painting called "The Ocean" over my desk.

The title helps
the wind and memory help the unappeasable
waves breaking up the beach the lilac sky and blue dunes

easily mistaken for
collapsed buildings or the loosened
clot of placenta the flowery scent inside the body her face

opening serene
as a goddess without portfolio
the wind stripping a twisted wing in the sand she ran

away from me
down the beach how the violet
waves break chasing my days a turmoil of jokes and hope

she cannot hear me
calling her name the waves scouring
their gaudy colors splashed over the page I can see where

she dragged her
finger through the red paint
and touched it to her lips the taste of salt chalk and iron.

WHY

Tonight my daughter is teaching me
the life of Vincent Van Gogh she knows it
from school quiet in the story circle the artist holding

a gun to his chest
her teacher turned the book to show them
his paintings so like their own the oils goopy smooshy

his self-portrait
in orange and aquarium green his jaw
bristly like her father's the cypresses writhing the road

a sloping nervous
torrent of daubs and dashes
she is six and knows why he did it *since my last attack*

I sense a loneliness
even in the open air he did it
because his pictures looked weird so nobody wanted them

she calls to me
in the morning her covers torn away
her room filled with the salmon and barium yellow of dawn

his window ajar
in the room at Arles the floor a sea-green
swell lifting the bed a room with no one there to see it

I am now
quite absorbed by the vast plain
the subtle yellow the soft green and violet under a sky

of delicate blue
white pink and lilac tones I am
in a mood of nearly too great calmness to paint this.

SNAIL

A tongue crossing the place where we burn
our trash the snail glides over
ashes nails and glass
moving by rhythmic contractions of its muscular foot
dragging its lungs and stomach in a clockwise-spiraling shell.

It stops
seeming to listen
waving its blind horns
then goes on remembering by touch
the way to the compost glazing the path with a glistening
slime the ground beneath it sealed
in a kind of sleep. The snail

does not hurry. Finding food it inserts its tooth-studded tongue
and rasps. Intertwined all day and night it performs
its delicate hermaphroditic copulation. Then sleeps
as if dead. It creeps

into our inner ear a coiled labyrinth
rooted to the brain.
We hear birds.
We hear the chirp of radio emissions from the heart
of the Milky Way a hundred billion stars in a slow snail whorl.
We hear the baby cry.

THREE | **IMPERSONATIONS**

OVID 101

You and your love-
wounds and metastasizing empire
your dubiety and (you'll have to admit it) disastrous advice

giving them ideas
my forty kids learning *you* Ovid see
you made it after all their faces agog or aghast or are they

just flummoxed
awash in giddiness and despair
how she hangs back after class to talk I can almost hear you

snicker you
swaggering macaroni just look at this
trouble you've made it's all your fault you and your many-

splendored gods
the quad sun-flooded abuzz
her voice (you would have said) *like music in the air*—OK

I'll write it
but in *my* measure not your clotted
hexed pentameters but these quick whiplash triplets the first

line breathless
then a rustle of wings spilling out
a long tumbling exhalation probing the margin of possibility

she touches my arm
thoughtfully but we talk of *you*
master dancing in the dark always you in exile nothing but

you serpent saint
of end-times and the shuddering
transformations of the body into a deer or a flowering tree.

LORENZO LOTTO
1480–1556

Qualmish
prickly the work sporadic
the paint insistent meticulous the glance of the sitter

vexed as if
the veil protecting his life
had been torn away your paintings weirdly lighted often

from below
a rebus of mysterious words
held aloft by the angels your mind *troubled by various*

odd apprehensions
a nervous yearning language of
emblems hieroglyphs ideograms and images of bewildering

semantic richness
a shudder of fear running through
the virgin's room the feathery hiss of an inrushing spirit

life stirring
in her womb scorned impoverished
you sold your belongings in 1527 and returned to Venice

the compositions
bizarre and intuitive whole
years of your life from which not a sketch remains *I am*

become forgetful
a lyrical lament issuing from
daily life a face at the center of a circle of gestures.

DÜRER'S PILLOW

1493

The artist took for his subject
six pillows

separate plumped
and dented forms as when
we first awaken and lift our heads leaving them warm

in the bunched
folds a face appears wherever
he looked he saw the human in all things a serene face

rinsed in prayer
or a face braying its lips peeled back
or the compressed face of a man lost in thought the face

radiantly smiling
or pierced and riven blurting
the small words seized chewing on its tongue the pillows

caved and crumpled
by the weight of his head a self-
portrait the eye skewed the cheek already hatched the ink

filling the sac
under his eye the sighting of land
the undefiled place the pillow printed with a human face.

JOSEPH OF COPERTINO
1603–1645

Featherbrained
thinking you had "slept a little"
you rose out of the pew into the air waving the beautiful

sea urchin
"stirred" as Bernino put it
in his magisterial *Vita* a lurching burbling child called

Open Mouth
your sudden flights announced
by a gasp or cry—*solito stridore*—the guttural squeal

of an imbecile
spinning wildly in circles then
breathing out a great sigh flying to the top of the altar

where you hovered
"for a quarter of an hour" your face
close to Mary like a child nuzzling and kissing his mother

what to believe
about your flying your oddness
and doubts your growing sense of spiritual defect how you

seized by the hair
a demented nobleman and cured him
rising aloft lifting him terrified off his feet charged

with dark arts
and spiritual fraud you suffered
a "short but difficult" interrogation and were released

to your cell
they kept you hidden entranced
airborne your eyes crossed your sandals hitting the floor.

JOHN CHAPMAN
1774–1845

The human murmur
hear it? What were they saying
their voices burbling what seemed to be the angel horde

of Emanuel Swedenborg
the dead are like us only happier
your father a Minuteman gone to engage the enemy at Lexington

your mother freezing
and sweating the bough about to break
into flower the larder dwindling the farm foreclosed gazing

West you saw
hell in the seething settlements
what we might become—treeless fruitless your mother dead

in appletime
your head crushed by the kick
of a horse the doctor drilled and drained your swollen skull

into a pan
a scar across your eye leaving you
sleepless troubled by dreams hearing the speech of animals

you set off
whistling over the snow freeing yourself
of your hat and coat barefoot ridiculous unhinged with your

battered Bible
a sack of seeds and a mushpot
on your head a boy (the story goes) shouting in the woods.

LOUIS BRAILLE
1809–1852

The book opens
your hand touching the page
finds the first word and begins to read how you stabbed

at a scrap of leather
with your father's awl it
jumped piercing your eye *a tragedy for one little boy*

it says here
but a boon for mankind the wound
itched and you rubbed the infection into your good eye

extending your arm
touching the lumpy relief map
at the Institute for the Young Blind their bright pupil

bird-boned
your high spiritual forehead
and small cough tracking the winding course of the Seine

into the Alps
you traced the raised bumps
of your letters made in the dark while the others slept

like a rash
on the page your fingers flying
gasping on the stair your death passed without notice

later exhumed
and reburied in the Pantheon
except for the bones of your hands sealed in a small urn.

DIARY OF AGNES STEWART

JUNE 11, 1862

Beyond the river
the territory stretches before me
nothing but trees as far as the eye can reach O Martha

we have begun
walking more than ever I did
waiting on the oxen to pull our wagon up the beautiful

green hills
like home if we had a house
today I can govern myself but not always trying to write

while walking
is it in my nature to love you
or because I have no other we cannot breathe for the smell

of dung made
8 miles and found our flour spoiled
camped at a place where a woman was buried the wolves

had dug her up
her hair was there with a comb in it
we should be grateful but the horses are lost I don't know

what to do yet
the horses are found again Mother
a little better Dear Martha I have not wrote for so long I

forget to know
how I feel I want to say
life to me is a dream of rocks and hollows we have come to

a perplexing lake
I will sit here with my diary
and think and never trouble to open it till time is past.

FRONTIER CLOCKMAKER

How short our time
wrestling the log grab and drag
shackle the buck saw maul and wedge splitting a wet plank

he can read
the scrawl of pith and grain
his workbook of Patience Obedience Determination each tool

worn to his palm
the adze mallet and chisel
pull-plane and ripsaw crashing in the wagon over mountain

and river *time*
and chance happeneth to them all
he carves and whittles the pinions and crown wheel fixed

to its verge
advancing one gear tooth
with each swing of the pendulum his wife stoops hauling

the bucket up
from the creek dragging her hem
through the cheat grass and camas her hips and shoulders

swaying he bends
the crutch wire *what is our life*
we are a mist that appears for a while and then vanishes

aligning the lift
dog and hammer shafts the heart
a bucket of pebbles pulling down he nudges the pendulum

its click clack
marking time the crawling hands
will keep our going out and coming in from this day forth.

JOSEPH MASON
1807–1883

Thin as a stick
you step from the *Journal* a boy of 13
in damp clothes Audubon's botanical assistant and starveling

the birds painted
then plucked and roasted "Joseph
Draws Flowers all day . . ." a stillness clinging to the flesh

of a petal
the settlers feverish murdering
a neighbor but little more than to kill a deer or a raccoon

his nervy black-
billed cuckoos pursuing a wasp
through your leaves and light his striving and griping his

"Sore eyes
and Violent Headaches" shooting them
wiring into place and drawing the birds still warm they land

on the sprig of
Magnolia grandiflora you provided
a place to preen and fidget the words "Plant by Jos. Mason"

all but erased
your unsung garden inhabited
by the 430-odd *Birds of America* Audubon consumed by doubts

debts and wrangling
his dazzling birds twisting in mid-
flight through your limbs never mentioned again you surface

in Cincinnati
where your career sputters your love
succumbs to fever you refuse to marry another and die at 76.

BAILEY AT SEA
1847–1906

Tidy polite
a small man buying a new lion
tallying the gate reckoning cashflow inventory payroll

reckoning desire
you led the Grand Diurnal Parade
Savage Animals in Open Lairs Freaks Fakes and Oddities

your strange ark
sailing with a crack company
and large menagerie to Australia heaving in a squall

the tiger's cage
slamming into and overturning the bears
squealing in terror the rhinoceros plunged overboard

the giraffe dead
(you have it skinned and stuffed
a mechanism inserted the head nodding gently on its neck)

bent on success
we know you suffered
an absence inside Jimmy McGinnes orphaned at seven

adopted by Fred Bailey
and the Robinson & Lake Wagon Show
you never looked back you never stopped running away

with the circus
your merger with Barnum trumpeted
a torchlit procession in the Marvelous Allegorical Car

20,000 in the tent
and thousands turned away you died
resplendent bewildered felled by the bite of an insect.

OZ

L. FRANK BAUM IN ABERDEEN
1856–1919

White hands
white gloves and ebony cane
you bring the lawn party and croquet to the frontier you

hate it *the gray*
everywhere the gray house and sky
the rutted roads and rickety sheds the plodding stolid

settlers you bring
the rose and the ventriloquist
you want all the meat from the nut of life opening

Baum's Bazaar
purveyor of the finest tinware
candy and ice cream bicycles cuspidors bonnets and frocks

every good thing
to make a little girl happy
we must foster year-round consumer desire your windows

bewitching
narrowing the eye vanishing
monkeys and frolicking leprechauns *anything to arouse*

their cupidity and longing
to possess the goods you give us
a live mannequin adorned with diamonds Haviland china

and miniature
typewriters haunted by failure
(chased by a scarecrow through your childhood nightmare)

you guide us
over the Deadly Desert to the Land
of Plenty where no one is feckless or wounded or numb.

HEINRICH MÜLLER
1865–1930

A summary of the case
of Heinrich Anton Müller of Munsingen
little is known of his early years working in a vineyard

when a change
took place in him he "invented"
a mechanism for harvesting grapes he began wandering about

aimlessly
neglecting his family at the time
of his committal claimed to be making millions he scraped

a large hole
in the garden to hide in he
constructed a helmet from flowers wire and tin cans

but mostly
he assembled a wobbly "machine"
an intricate fretwork of gears and pulleys he bent

and lashed together
from supple switches and saplings
forming a cage in which the engine a coiling of vines

thrummed as if
it were dreaming itself
a dynamo its axles and flywheels chirping like birds

he manipulated
a lever to guide its holy work
maintaining the operations of the eternal in our world.

JANIS JOPLIN
THE TYPEWRITER TAPE
1943–1970

Hit play
and your injured voice goes on
without you sweeping along the debris of memory nowhere

more than here
on this bootleg tape laid down
in the crowded apartment you are present raw inevitable

not yet drunk
but on your way a wavery blue
wall of noise crashing from the amps it doesn't matter

the phone ringing
the dog barking while you sing
through the daily sounds of who we were a distant siren

a typewriter
in the next room someone
pecking out the letters writing a paper we were students

after all
we hardly noticed the brittle
mechanical chatter like locusts like an argument

we were going
to lose the heart singing along
with the music but the machine keeping up with the mind.

APPARITION

Music of voices
on the street music in the form
of oranges or kisses it could happen to anyone a middle-aged

man stumbles
on the walk ahead of me spilling
his paper bag of clamps glue and screws he must be going home

to fix something
whatever it was he touched
and broke he looks up and I see it's my dead friend but how

can that be
I help him stand and straighten
his rumpled clothes his cheeks ashen creased raspy traffic

music or is it
the greasy throb of work turbines
braying in the sky spirits in flight he's been gone so long

he's changed
which is only to be expected his coat
silky glimmering who used to find his clothes in the freebox

and he's calmer
almost peaceful now who used to hurl
curses stoning the police awash in hate and love and terror

wan polite he waits
for the light to change his hand
beginning to twist who used to gnash who used to burn and burn.

FOUR | **BIRDMAN**

In the end there is no longer a wing hooked to a framework but a form flawless in its perfection, completely disengaged from its matrix, a sort of spontaneous whole, its parts mysteriously fused together and resembling in their unity a poem.

—ANTOINE DE SAINT-EXUPÉRY, "THE TOOL"

BIRDMAN

Cast into the air
I chirped from memory spreading
my arms my body floating over the yard over the lilacs

crying out then
plunging into my father's embrace
we shall begin with an account of its flight the Oval Body

propelled by rapid
wingbeats and steered by a long
well-plumed tail a bird gliding through the woods passes

like a thought
his father whistles tremolos
and sweetly plausible warblings they listen for the birds

to answer a man
with wings attached to his arms
leapt from a cliff and was dashed on the roof of the Temple

of Apollo flying
above the earth in the open firmament
of heaven Wild Pigeons stream through our American woods

in Countless Multitudes
their backs a glistening torrent
of azure their suddenly presented purple breasts sweeping

close to the ground
and rising in a vast Column
echoes of God's dress and manner in the shape and color

of birds
having discovered the flying
elixir a cloudy flux of cinnabar and sulfur Lui-an drank

and rose dropping
the vessel to the ground where
his dogs and chickens sipped the dregs and followed him

into the sky
the shallow lagoons and flats
of viscous calcareous mud where storms blew in flowers

insects pterosaurs
and archaeopteryx a fine silt
sliming the eye the feathers' compressed and fractured

imprint of memory
Chorus [within]: Tórotorotórotix toto-
tĭx Whit tuwhít tuwhít Tórotorotórotorolílilíx Pigeons

arrive by the Thousands
a scene of Torches and Slaughter guns
and sticks striking them out of the air a great Clatter

the ground covered
with the dead and mangled Hundreds
wandering about in wild confusion their cervical vertebrae

elongate and narrow
the coracoid is short and rounded
the acetabulum roofed above by the supercotabular buttress

the fibula
gracile compared with the tibia etc.
a Turk his sail-like billowy garment gathered into pleats

and folds fell
dead at the base of a high tower
the children trained from infancy in the art of flying

with artificial
wings allowing them to stride
with incredible speed skimming over the earth the unborn

chick twists
to face the blunt end of the egg
pecks the air sac and fills its lungs for the first time

the mother may
hear it calling inside the poet Po Ku-i
wore flying slippers embroidered with clouds and scented

with four perfumes
they rise up in a circling manner
during the Love Season his call a short *coo-ah* they caress

their simple nest
a few twigs crossed in a tree
they are killed in Great Numbers and yet they appear to us

undiminished his wings
made of wire hoops his helmet
an eagle with open beak João Torto leapt from the steeple

to his death a hole
appears in the egg and the chick
rests its bouts of pecking at the shell followed by periods

of stillness
a doctor from the quarry district
received an archaeopteryx as payment its head thrown back

wings splayed
a French laborer jumped
from a pear tree with winnowing baskets tied to his arms

a coal shovel
clasped between his legs fell
into a sewage drain and broke his shoulder they Walk with

Ease jerking
their beautiful tails and gliding
their necks backward and forward a man on a horse rose

under a balloon
amidst immense cheering they went up
at twenty minutes to eight the horse gazing down his eyes

fixed on the earth
a crack extends around the egg
the chick turning inside completing the circle it heaves

its shoulders lifts
the cap and tumbles out a featherless
rubbery lump a boy of twelve his long coat used as a wing

fell on a stone
and was emasculated these being
the four several ways whereby their flying hath been

attempted: (1) by spirits
or angels (2) by the help of fowls
(3) by wings fastened directly to the body (4) in a chariot

drawn by the power
of the passengers within Lu-pan
constructed a wooden kite mounted by his father who sailed

to Wu-hiu
a town in the prefecture of Su-chow
where he was taken by the people as a demon and slain

embryolike
its swollen abdomen a translucent
sack of veins its neck limp as a knotted rope it lifts

a stubby arm
twice failing a peasant with wings
of mica severely beaten by a crowd gathered to witness

his flight
the body is fastened to the girdle
the feet rest in stirrups (*mn*) passes beneath the arms and

twists the wings (*b*)
turns them with a lever (*c*) lowers them
(*d*) raises them responding to the least sound or jarring

of the nest
by thrusting up its head and opening
its mouth wide the men assemble under the nesting trees

with axes
the Squabs dashed to the ground
gathered in Immense Piles plucked and crated for market

the flying instrument
lacks nothing but the vigor
of the bird and this must be supplied by a man the life

principle and propeller
"Herr Genser was so kind as to
photograph me in the air high over the miller of Derwitz

(in whose barn
I stored my glider and apparatus)
and his esteemed poodle dog" fledged restless the nestlings

peer out
their parents gliding slowly past
exhorting them to fly for a week or so they fed on nothing

but the flesh of Pigeon
and talked of nothing but Pigeon its meat
of a dark color yet affords tolerable eating the feathers

fall off at the least
touch the clavicles fused to the V
of the furcula anchoring the massive pectoralis pulling

the wing down
for the power stroke this truant thought
that the problem of flight may be solved by man when once

the idea invades
his mind it possesses it entirely
it becomes his haunting his waking nightmare impossible to

shake the wind
failing confused the elevator
attached by cables and a harness to his forehead the glider

entered a steep
dive and crashed severing his spine
the oval walls of the fuselage curving up and around him

curiously comforting
and secure balancing intangible forms
the pilot erases terrestrial ugliness he reads and weighs

the stupendous
landscapes seascapes and skyscapes
intelligent industrious congenial [Lindbergh] the artist

expresses his mood
the sky a canvas stretched smooth
and still with a movement of his wrist the stick between

thumb and forefinger
as though it were a brush the plane
circles upward like a flicker of flame painted in the air

his eyes clear
his smile quick like a practiced
diplomat he eludes any entangling conversation near faint

or vertiginous
spell the momentary loss
of coordination or orientation a transient clouding of vision

"Why should one
spend the hours of his life on formulae
semicolons and our crazy English spelling I don't believe

God made man to fiddle
with pencil marks on paper He gave him
earth and air to feel and now even wings with which to fly"

from an early age
he began to believe that he could kill
with his penis *And he did teach his sonne how he should*

also flie
He fastened to his shoulders twaine
a pair of uncouth wings conveying pride prestige control

aggression
perfectionism inability to relax
tendency to avoid and deny emotions externalize conflicts

in depressive
and self-destructive behavior
the airman's profession is one of renunciation of women

in this way
he discovers his hidden god
loops spins barrel-rolls Lufbery circles cross-over turns

Jenny Immelmanns
figure-eights wing-overs and reversements
chandelles vertical banks and split-air turns in speed

we are hurled
beyond ourselves our bodies cannot
scale the heavens except in a fume of petrol *we enter it*

we come the flyers
clutching their charms a champagne cork
a scarf made from the parachute of a dead friend recalling

the 3-year-old
with a toy animal in bed about to face
the darkness in a flash of speed and smoke the young men

pass with a cry
and a gesture and are gone
pursuit and attack observation and bombardment formation

dogfights strafing
gunnery on ground targets shadow
and tow targets on the Lewis turret-mounted and Browning

synchronized-through-
the propeller at 1,200 rounds/min.
Picadilly Commando Messy Bessy My Angel Violent Virgin

Heavenly Body
we measure heroes as we do ships
by their displacement Col. Lindbergh displaces everything

he lifts us
into the freer and upper air
that is his home he displaces all things sordid or vulgar

seeing his bombs
falling on their target the bombardier
cannot contain himself he jumps up and down in his seat

like a happy child
hit by flak the plane in front explodes
what he takes for a piece of debris flying back is their

gunner who strikes
the Number Two propeller splatters
over the windshield and freezes there a moment of fear

then no particular
conscious feeling persists
but all emotional content is screened by the ego and stored

under strong repression
study pilot coping strategies
generate a model of occupational stress the impact of grief

underlying trends
and event data he remembers
his nursery window open to the waves a huge sea bird

sheered over
his cradle striking him starting him
rocking crazed with terror the dark bird circled his room

the arm opens
the elbow joint extends the wrist
stretches the primary feathers spread in flying position

he lifted the lamb
and after caressing it awhile
threw the animal aloft and followed after it into the air

over the trees
where he remained suspended
in ecstasy for a quarter of an hour his arms open wide

I flew out
of my father's hands a human form
rigid against the sky we enter a zone of snowy whiteness

red footprints
on the floor of the fuselage
we declare that wings are asleep in the flesh we yearn

we climb
into the sky *So heartens he*
his little sonne to follow teaching him a hurtful Art.

FIVE | **WEEDS**

THE HEART

I hang up
and the room resumes its silence.
Travelers gather at the bottom of the Chinese landscape

one halters
a pack mule another touches
the buttons on his tunic or is he asking his heart

are you ready
the arched bridge the quick brush-
flicks of bamboo the path twisting along a steep ridge

one gazes
woozily down into the ravine
the mists and riffles and drop-offs like the wet inside

of his chest
the heart keeps pumping it won't
stop for anything even taken from the body it goes on

beating the path
climbs past the partly hidden stone
temple inked on the golden silk the travelers arrive

cloaked in dust
at the cliff edge one seems
about to gather his robes and step off into the clouds.

RECONCILIATION

No letter no word
for weeks then the phone it's you Lois
in the distance your voice thinned windblown the pouchy

grapes or plums
of lymphoma you're praying
again opening to Genesis where Jacob is fording the Jabbok

still afraid
after twenty years returning
home to Esau his witless twin he snookered tussling even

in the womb
tangled in the wrinkled scarf
of umbilical finding himself wrestling it may be an angel

a poor prognosis
we find ourselves in need of words
more heavy-muscled and cunning what cannot be spoken

except like this
sudden halts registering the small
dislocations of thought the angel cool scentless his wing

wrenched back
you wake up needing to vomit unlike
Jacob in the dark unlike the angel releasing him at dawn

and blessing him
who seems to be gleaming even Esau
sees and falls on his neck and kisses him weeping for joy.

SHOO

A far cry
we're listening over the bed lost
for words a fly faintly grinds and crunches on the ceiling

a plague spot
on your pillow you sweep it away
spiraling over the window scumbling the glass is it sleep

coming on
or the shimmery medication the red
leaves curling the plums thickening the bus taking a turn

too wide swaying
the riders in their seats the fly
on the sill the spoon crawling on your sleeve you say get

off me fly
shaking the water glass flashes
in the sunlight our lives with such excruciating too-late

beauty swell
the fly on your hand you watch it
yearning downy eagerly touching you with its mouthparts.

BILLIARDS AFTER THE SERVICE

Your turn
to lean over the table and break
the pool balls coming to rest a constellation

not a game
to hurry through it lets us
not speak Brother finding an easy shot you

pocket it
striking others on the ricochet
like the beads of a rosary scattered on the floor

a star appears
over the motel then others smaller
or just farther off we drove away from the open grave

a diaspora
the way blocked the faint
sizz of a ball spinning in place like a bright planet

a tricky bank
a lot of English and the gentlest
possible cuff of stone on stone starting it rolling even

our atoms
strewn over the soft green
each ball hushed toward the dark falling with a tunk.

TRUCK

I shall now
praise my neighbor's truck
crouched on its slab black and metallic candy-apple red

emblazoned
with chevrons and swashes of gold
his only chariot why shouldn't he treasure it glistening

like unto
the color of beryl the mirrored
grillwork and foglights on the roof the little trumpets

of annunciation
the leaping trout and bull elk
the eagle airbrushed wheeling over a mountain lake

who can tell
the shape a dream might take
the appearance of animals round about within it moving

in a cloud
of exhaust the waterfall spilling
over a fender a great plain spanning the hood the desert

silhouette and deep
ocean all the world the likeness
of the firmament and its weather why shouldn't he cherish

this his ark
his rescue carrying him forth turning
neither right nor left but whither the spirit might go.

THIS BEING

the end she's off
behind the wheel driving herself
to the airport looking for the exit trying to make language

describe her
powdery flesh the glass and chrome
flashing on the cars climbing the ramp to the terminal pigeons

scatter
from the alcoves bearing right then
under the overpass losing then finding her way again the way

blocked enter
here for outgoing flights circling
back do not enter her thoughts turning to God the ultimate

unreliable narrator
her life unraveling how she drives
all this way only to discover how shabby it gets at the end

not like her
first flight over the cornfields
rapt sobbing the propellers shaking the foil the birds fly

up clouding her
sight feathers and wings needing
in the words more thought and suddenness more tension more

clarity her fate
after all is before us her plane
waiting to take her wind and light mingling on the runway.

TEN REASONS TO DREAD THE WIND

One it rouses us
touching us all over the cool
puff of wind then a stillness we hold our breath

sure enough two
it's back pulling at us plucking
our hair tugging at our clothes our flesh it blows our hats off

three it crumples
the surface of the lake it surges
over the town streaming around our lives a rumpus a turmoil

four listen
it speaks a raspy voice saying
think thou upon the wondrous works of God the ruinous wind

the cyclone five
the hot katabatic wind shriveling
the wispy grass *for surely man is grass* yet six it cannot be

seen no one
is safe seven it shrieks wrecking
the house leaving the sofa a dirt-spattered wall it lifts us

eight we are
scattered over the land nine
it casts our words these torn scraps of sound into the air

ten the wind
yearns through us filling our mouths
the air searing our lungs gasping and gulping like newborns.

RESTORATION

A woman crosses
the stage cradling her violin she
trips on a sound wire gravity takes over and she falls

it happens.
The violin is crushed beneath her
its strings limp slithery coiled in a nest of splinters

the purpled
reverberations of G silent as God
the shouts and father-voice of D the mother crooning in A

and the infant shriek and zingy giggle on the E string
all hushed she feels herself rising
one of the pegs

like a fetus
lost in the folds of her black skirt.
But this is not about endings. Here the violin is restored

each fragment
retrieved and returned to its place
the ribs meticulously fitted glued and clamped the neck

and shoulder purfling and fingerboard the arched belly
and back the waist and scroll
the face

crazed a lacework
of cracks the voice a sonorous
groaning in the lower register the high notes edgy reckless.

WHIM

Recycled paper
flecked with post-consumer waste
this pocked and freckled page on which to describe a woman

with *whim*
tattooed on her shoulder in wobbly cursive
from Emerson (she thought) *Who would be a person must be*

a nonconformist.
I would write over the doorway
Whim the paper stippled with lint rags and bandages

shredded books
loosened in the soupy acid bath
steaming vats pouring out the fibrous slurry the stainless

rollers extruding
the paper wide as a bedsheet
spangled with blood and semen and milk the sweet stigmata

of human use
this fleshy page on which to write out
our lives *I hope it is something more than whim at last.*

THE GIFT

Couldn't she tell
it was a joke you rose and
tapped your glass with a spoon and when there was silence

addressed her
remembering how young and poor
when you met you had promised her one day a rock to wear

on her finger
you hoped it wasn't too late
placing the perfectly wrapped white satin box in her hand

it was heavy
she opened it slowly and held
the smooth greenish river stone in her palm her face lit

turning it over
and over it was just a prank
the diamond was in your pocket a gleaming ice chip locked

in the jaws
of the ringbox she noticed a white
cloud of quartz passing over the stone you'd picked it up

on the driveway
warming like an egg in her palm
she thought then for a moment she'd married the right man

after all
and kissed you her long kiss
deeper and more complex than any you'd ever known before.

NEARLY ASLEEP I REMEMBER

the boy's cheek
dense as a waxed apple a black
field of mint flying past on the cusp of sleep a rickety

fruit stand
a watermelon cut open to show
the ripeness inside the murmurs and perfume the crowd

eddying around
his casket shuffling across
the gangplank the engines thrumming through our bodies

a dreamy
boy the fog horn bleating
from the shore there was no turning back his serene

face in the flowers
in an unfamiliar bed the wind
pulling at our hair and clothes trying to pull us apart

the boat
rocked the wake boiled
the children horsed around on the slippery upper deck

the whiskered faces
of seals watching us pass I almost
slept then I thought of the harbor opening to receive us

I remembered him
playing the cello the sudden thump
of landing everyone thrown off balance and then I slept.

SWITCHYARD

I'm awake again with the shrill singing
in my ears. Another world
must begin at the end of our road
the empty boxcars coupling and uncoupling
their steel wheels ringing where they squeeze the track.

A boy I listened
with the box turtle and the crickets my sister was
raising the flute to her lips trying
for the high clear notes.

I heard the boats
returning to harbor loaded with mackerel
with panic the fisherman tired of his work all day
reaching into the water— the winch squealed lifting
the big bucket up out of the hold.

I'm lying still in the dark
still awake, still in love. If I rise
and leave in the direction of these sounds I'll come
to the tracks a locomotive moving this way and that selecting
cars like words in a sentence. I'll find the homeless
huddled under a trestle.

I'll have my whole life there with me.
If they ask for a little change
I'll give it to them.

PARACHUTE

The worm weaves
rapturous parabolas the flesh
dances in its silk casting a luminous thread from its mouth

but the house
unravels the girl reeling in
the filament a half-mile to the crusted lip of the chrysalis

she twists and throws
the lacy weft of tissue stitched
under pressure swivels and grommets the seams reinforced

at the D-ring
she is careful positioning the webs
and tendons coiling the lines into the pack gathering up

the silvery tucks
and pleats like a wedding gown veil
upon veil it must emerge and disentangle at the first tug

the ground
rushing toward us the body
trailing its white silk like a collapsed wing or afterbirth.

HOME

Returning to earth after his life
of weightlessness the astronaut cannot
lift the small bouquet of flowers the child gives him.
He cannot raise his head off the pillow pulled down
by the gravity of a dream.

He remembers nothing no sound
in the absolute zero of deep space
the pounding of his baffled heart. He lifted
a building in one hand and a pencil in the other.
This was what he wanted: the world

like a worn stone cast into the water.
He wanted to break the promise of the body
to the earth. To stop the long descent of everyone
he loved under the ground. He wanted to rise an angel
in a paradise of exact data.

He spills his milk on his shirt. The earth
has darkness and then light. The earth has birds
bickering over the last seeds. His fork slips
clattering on the plate. The road is shining.
The magnolia is shameless in the rain.

IT WASN'T THAT

A tree fell
in the wind it wasn't that
we had a clear sense of where our lives were taking us

it wasn't that
something wasn't missing or that
we had much of a choice you see what I'm saying it wasn't

that we failed
to notice the pale wash of light
rosy on the bedroom wall how we touched the flesh quaking

with happiness how
the heart swung open it wasn't
that we didn't love the wind we were like wind ourselves

we got in
and drove we felt hurried
swept along by the surge of time we couldn't say why

the sky quickened
and flashed the water busied itself
the child reached out her pudgy hands it wasn't easy

to say it
wasn't that we didn't try or that
looking back we would have done anything differently

we settled into
our lawn chairs it wasn't that
we didn't enjoy ourselves we had a pretty good time.

ACKNOWLEDGMENTS

My thanks to my sister, Janet Poskas, for her courage and inspiration.
Thanks also to Deb Casey, my first and best reader; to Linda Bierds,
Gretchen Van Meter, and Marilyn Trueblood at the University of
Washington Press; and to the editors of the following publications,
where these poems originally appeared:

American Poetry Review: "Switchyard"
Antioch Review, "Grace"
Iowa Review: "Captivity," "The Heavenly Ladder"
Massachusetts Review: "The Sound Barrier"
New England Review: "Likeness" (originally "Breast Poem")
The New Yorker: "Home"
Notre Dame Review: "Fugue for Josie," "Restoration" (originally "Violin")
Ohio Review: "Naming" (originally "Anna")
Ontario Review: "Helicopter Ride" (originally "Chopper"), "Swath,"
   "Why"
Paris Review: "Snail"
Prairie Schooner: "John Chapman," "Louis Braille"
Shenandoah, "Iris Innominata"
Virginia Quarterly Review: "Apparition"

"Switchyard" was reprinted in *Wherever Home Begins: 100 Contemporary
Poems*, Orchard Books, 1995.

"Home" was reprinted in *The Norton Introduction to Literature*, 4th ed.,
1986; *The Norton Introduction to Poetry*, 3rd ed., 1986; *In the Age of the
Smart Machine: The Nature of Work and Power*, Basic Books, 1988;
and *Late for the Sky: The Mentality of the Space Age*, Southern Illinois
University Press, 1992.

"Nearly Asleep I Remember" is for Bill and Lynne Rossi,
in memory of Joel.

ABOUT THE POET

John Witte's poems have appeared in *The New Yorker*, *Paris Review*, *American Poetry Review*, and, among several anthologies, *The Norton Introduction to Literature*. The recipient of two fellowships from the National Endowment for the Arts, he lives with his family in Eugene, Oregon, where he teaches at the University of Oregon. *Second Nature* is his third collection of poems.

A NOTE ON THE TYPE

FF Meta Serif, completed in 2007, was designed collaboratively by German type designer Erik Spiekermann, American type designer Christian Schwartz, and New Zealand type designer Kris Sowersby. It was developed to serve as a counterpart for the humanist san serif typeface, FF Meta, created in 1985 by Erik Spiekermann.

The poetry is set in 9.5 pt FF Meta Serif Book with 14 pt leading. Poem titles are set in FF Meta Bold 11.5 pt with 14 pt leading. The typesetting was done by Ashley Saleeba.